Poems Written While Not Studying at Harvard

Poems Written While Not Studying at Harvard

Jamie Zwiebel

iUniverse, Inc.
Bloomington

Poems Written While Not Studying at Harvard

iUniverse books may be ordered through booksellers or by contacting:

iUniverse
1663 Liberty Drive
Bloomington, IN 47403
www.iuniverse.com
1-800-Authors (1-800-288-4677)

ISBN: 978-1-4620-1775-1 (pbk)
ISBN: 978-1-4620-1776-8 (ebk)

Library of Congress Control Number: 2011907143

Printed in the United States of America

iUniverse rev. date: 06/24/2011

CONTENTS

Foreword

The power of procrastination.

I actually *did* study at Harvard. Lots. But obviously, while I was writing these poems, I wasn't studying for my Master's of Science in Public Health. No, I was thinking about things people don't talk (much) about, those between-the-lines things which usually live as unspoken thoughts that few people can find time to share, much less listen to themselves.

These poems are evidence of just how much I procrastinated as a graduate student, but also how much I learned. They're about things people don't tend to talk about, but that doesn't make them any less true.

Poems written in Harvard Yard (either on the yard, or in the library instead of studying)

"Take a minute to feel sorrow for the folks who think tomorrow is a place that they can call up on the phone. Spend a month and show some kindness to the folks who thought that blindness was an illness that affected eyes alone."-Maya Angelou

Things People Don't Talk About

What happens in the bathroom
or the zone between your thighs
Why the world is run
by rich white guys
God's role the market
(He's in disguise)

No room for Him
at the Wall Street Inn
Most precious unit of true currency
turned to the margins
of "modern" society

God lives in the silence
in between the lines
of the lies that we tell
to pretend that we're fine

God lives in the moments
between you and I
like free-flowing water
becoming fine wine

God lives in the silence
when we pause the lies
and in the white noise of pretension
He dies

Mad Hatter Men

I am very important
Very important
Very, very, very important

I can't cook or clean;
I've got to trade stocks
and break locks
and train jocks
cause I'm very important

I can't stop my habits
of boozing and looting
and cheating and shooting
cause I'm very important

I can't watch the kids
cause the Celtics are on
and Iran has the bomb
and it's very important

I can't change the diapers;
we all know ass-wipers
are people who aren't really
very important

I quench my desires
with the smoldering pyres
of triple x domains and
the sharp silent pains

of whores behind doors
held by johnnys who wink
and odors that reek
of sex and mystique
cause my needs are very
very important

The world would end now if
I didn't run 'round with
my suits and salutes and
my black combat boots cause
I am the man who
runs this whole land and I'm
very, very, very important

Game Theory

oh economic sociology
with its models and game theories
players and strategies
vertexes
matrices
pretend rationality
homogeneity
convenient parsimony
academic utility
oligarchs playing
parcheesi with destinies
freeriding on
labor they call
externalities
selectively crafting
endogenous
market entries and
exits at the nexus
of myopic audacities
if only john nash and his beautiful mind could see
how we spend our days in these hallowed halls of ivy

Birthright Africa

Overview:

Birthright West Africa provides the gift of first time, peer group, educational trips to West Africa for young adults of African descent ages 18 to 26. Birthright West Africa's founders created this program to send thousands of young people from all over the African Diaspora to Africa as a gift in order to diminish the growing division between the African continent and African Diaspora communities around the world; to strengthen the sense of solidarity among people of African descent, and to strengthen participants' personal African identity and connection to the continent. All trips will launch from Ghana, the former Gold Coast and the center of British slave trade for more than 150 years, where participants will visit key sites along the Slave Route Project of the United Nations Educational, Scientific and Cultural Organization (UNESCO), including trading posts such as Cape Coast and Elmira Castles. Trip itineraries will then vary according to each trip's focus and may include visits to the sites of the Anglo-Ashanti wars and to the Bight of Biafra from which European slave traders took 15% of the 10 million people traded, most of whom were Igbo, and tracing the steps of Usman dan Fodio, founder of the Fulani Empire.

Partners:

The gift of the 14-day trip is being provided by our partners: private philanthropists through The Birthright West Africa Foundation; the people of West Africa through the governments of Benin, Burkina Faso, Cape Verde, Cote d'Ivoire, The Gambia, Ghana, Guinea, Guinea-Bissau, Liberia, Mali, Mauritania, Niger, Nigeria, Senegal, Sierra Leone, and Togo, and African Diaspora communities around the world, especially the African-North American Federation and the African-American Agency for Africa. Please take a few minutes to learn more about our partners, especially your local African Federation, which is your gateway to community involvement, continued learning and leadership opportunities.

- The Birthright West Africa Foundation Executive Committee includes Oladayo Olowo, Chair, Ife Garma, Vice Chair, Opeyemi Osuntogun, Treasurer/Vice Chair, Nweke Johnson, Secretary, Akwasi Mensah, ex-oficio, Djidé Foula, Okorie Thompson, Coumba Soto, ex-oficio, and Sami Diop.

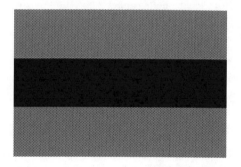

- This educational program has been supported by a grant from the Conference on African Diaspora Material Claims Against Former Colonial Slave-Masters, with chapters throughout the United States, Latin America, and Western Europe, which works to spur investment and mutual uplift in the Diaspora after 500 years of systematic impoverishment and exploitation.

Frozen Orange

"I hold a frozen orange."-Jordanian rape survivor

Frozen orange,
sweet and secret
sorrow in my freezer.

Feeling neither cold nor heat,
I touch you.
You shock me with your
frozen hardness.

I bite with no shame,
knowing I deserve
the sweetness of your
primal tang.

Oh holy nectar,
given unto me.
Orange volcanic eruption,
paralyzing empty rage fades
by the power of your earthly fruit.

Oh glorious rush of orange lava,
oh secret freezer stash of sanity.
Citrus balm to my bleary, blinking soul,
anchor from the inert gray ashen waters of my spirit,

how many of my kind will hold an orange now
in their hands

alone in their kitchens, adrift in vacant galaxies of despair,
steadied by the gravitational force of a tiny, frozen, orange sun,
that elemental remembrance of the here and now.

How many hold a frozen orange now
with the desperate clutch of unrecognized sojourners
who have been to coasts and with their toes touched the gray and
brackish tides of hell.

How many lean over their sinks, taking slow breaths,
savoring the icy yet sweet harbor from their daily storms,
awash in the gray purgatory of their secrets,
with only their fruit to comfort them.

The Worry

Always worrying about what people think of me,
treating God like She's just another person judging me,
making the whole world about their thoughts of me.
Help me not to want what is not mine to have.

Oh this vast delusion of entitlement.
Were I unworthy, I would not even be present.
But I'm still chasing after self-esteem; acclaim is just a pipe
dream.
It's all about the only One who "gets" me.

It's all about faith in the gifts She gives me.
I relapse into voyeuristic tendencies,
escaping so I don't have to face my potential,
and the fact that even I'm somehow essential
to a world where we're all interdependent,
a world where no one needs constant reminding
of their brokenness, a world of holy living words, spoken divinely
into being.
So tell me why I can't seem to stop worrying.

Distract Distract Distract

Hold it in hold it in
Hold it in
Hold it in
Until you don't remember what you were holding in

Keep it down, keep it down
Keep it down
Keep it down
Until you forget what you were keeping down

Distract, distract
Distract
Distract
Until distraction becomes your reality

Lie, lie
Lie
Lie
Until falsehood becomes your truth

Until truth can't threaten lies
Until love can't conqueror fear

But then somebody said:
"What I have to say to you
is rebel.

Jamie Zwiebel

While today is still today,
choose well,
choose well,
choose well,
choose well."
-Lauryn Hill

And then I knew that
"Fear is internal,
Love is internal
Hell is internal."
-Maya Angelou

Look within and try
to remember.

"I see my beauty in you."
-Rumi

I Won't Bow

No, I will not own an iPhone.
No, I will not own a droid.
I'll just own the land I stand on.
Everywhere I go all mine.
No, I will not go on Facebook.
No, I won't use Microsoft.
Or Mac.
Or Google.
YouTube.
Twitter.
I'll just own my beautiful face.
The one inside you cannot see.
The one that cannot die or perish,
not like this cracking body.
I'll just accept the gift of living,
even if I have to die.
I won't pay you to make me happy.
No, cause that's too much a price.
I won't pay you to feed me, heal me.
No, I won't bow to your pride.
I'll just bow to the One who sent me.
It's all His; by His love, mine.

Radical Patience

I was so empty
running on empty
eating myself so devoted to emptiness
running out of time to consume the Divine
anecdote to my pain
How could I eat my bread when I was so enraged
at the mere idea of bowing to something other than
my ego
The more I trust my flesh the more it lets
me down
Again and again, but still I pretend
I know better
than the One who gives me all things
my Creator
Thinking that my clever words
trump the Savior's
Chasing after dying things,
my betrayer,
is this identity I've pegged
to the dollar,
fleeting moments of pleasure,
popular opinion
Choosing death over life
again and again
Trusting the enemy
like he's my friend

Writing this poem
as if it's not yet written
when all of our stories
are found in the Scripture
Oh holy words, oh imperfect reflections
these human arts
Mortal visions unclear
strain to see in each other
the true image of beauty
when all of society
runs with blinders on empty
When separate fates
join in one common destiny
complete in the story
that my Savior wrote for me

Clocks

My watch stopped working.
Then the ice cream parlor's clock
started to melt.
I couldn't see its
hands or numbers,
only something vaguely reminiscent
of a Dali painting.
When I asked people for the time they said: *wahhwahh,*
sort of like Charlie Brown's teacher's voice.
And then the TV stopped working.
Oh no! How will I watch reruns
of "Friends" and "The Office"?
Machines sputter and die at my touch.
I'm like King Midas on crack.
Great. The radio blares, irate
then stops mid-sentence (something about "Obamacare").
Reading the news is not so bad, paper in hand,
but when the internet blew out, I didn't know what to think
anymore.
Always wondering: *what's going on?*
What should I be doing?
What am I missing?
But soon I forgot, because then,
my credit card was denied, and the ATM

didn't seem to recognize
my pin number. I had my lucky hundred,
but once that was gone, I was so done.
I had nowhere to go, so I went to the street,
begging for money or something to eat.
Today I saw a building crumble, its gargoyles shrivel up
and die, the way petrified demons turn
to stone, and something worse,
too grave to speak of. Soon all of this will be
dust in the sea.
I can't read this new language all around me;
they pray to money, walk right by me
as if I had the plague. But I found something more important
than life.
Tonight a wave will rise up over the city,
like when a young boy plays at the shoreline,
watching his castles crumble instantly.
Then we will see that all idols are sand,
for what is stone? Even dollars bills don't float
that long. The sea swallows cars whole.
More efficient than any paper shredder
or trash compactor.
And really everything we see
is attached by string to the nose of a giant wakeboard
ridden by a tall thin man.
The redwoods are uprooted instantly
by the strength of this mysterious
string. Mountains skim the water's surface,
Lady Liberty on her side, swimming with Tapei Towers,
the London Eye, the Empire State, the White House Rotunda,
the Rose Garden, everything uprooted that was planted.

Jamie Zwiebel

The only hope is to grab onto something real today,
before the Wakeboarder comes to string us along,
so that we may drown and die to the puppetry
of slavery to invisible strings, so that our souls
will live on. That's why tonight
I'm holding onto my soul.
I don't need anything
but that which loves me whole.

Poems from Conversations with People in Central and Harvard Squares Asking for Goodwill

New employee to store manager: You want me to sweep? But I
have a college degree.

Manager to employee: Oh, I'm sorry, I forgot.
Let me show you how.

Augustine

He wears fur in late summer
and chats, in front of City Hall
with people no one else can see.
These are the signs of Augustine's fall.

He doesn't read, but speaks five tongues,
an American born Haitian,
but "from the sky" and so he knows
Spanish, Japanese, Creole . . .
It's a wonder his head doesn't explode!

His eyes glaze when I spell a word
or ask him of his mother.
He came straight from the sky, he says,
directly from the Father.

Sometimes he sleeps outside the bank
like he expects a call,
there underneath the public phone,
snoring soundly, sprawled.

He has a plane inside, he says;
the Father will be calling.
So he will take that trip back home.
It only looks like falling.

Sampson Samuel

I ask if you are Mexican;
you say you're an American,
born a Punjabi.
Whoops, I'm sorry.

You served in the army.
You killed a Somali.
Now no sleep or peace for you.
Sampson, I'm sorry.

Every minute of the day,
the searing pain won't go away.
You hold your head, you twitch and say
that you did wrong.
You killed a man, somebody's son.
No peace for you, Sampson.

Sampson, lying in the street,
so drunk with pain no bottle keeps
away. He say he knows that God forgives,
and still he wonders why he lives.

Sun burns his eyes, trapped in disguise,
a brown man who looks "Mexican",
served Uncle Sam in '91
and slurs his words as if he's drunk,

enduring being spat upon
for a few quarters in his cup.

Maybe his drunk; that's not enough
reason to pass, as if he's dead.
I tell him, as he holds his head,
"I'm sorry, Sampson."

Richie from Tennessee

The Chair came crashing down
from his mother's arms.

The Chair crashed, beat, and bruised his head.
And she apologized like the other times,
bought him ice cream, said she'd make it right.

Richie's angry, but not bitter;
he's met Dolly Parton twice.
He's only got one mother,
and he's only got one life.

The home for boys was Catholic,
now his church is Everywhere.
He sings beside the Charles,
with soft moss for his chair.

He's pretty lit from noon to night;
he'll be your friend if you don't care.

Richie from Tennessee,
with the kind eyes and the wild hair.

Richie from Tennessee,
the boy who escaped The Chair.

Andrea and Anuk

Andrea held Anuk too tight,
so he bit and scratched
(but he never bites)
and left a small gash in her chest.

"It's my fault" says Andrea.
"Anyone would bite
if held too tight."
Even darling grey-nosed
tabby Eskimos,
like Anuk.

Now Andrea's by the T stop,
perched atop a concrete block,
smiling in the starlight,
holding a moonlit cup.

Surgery ate the welfare check.
Pantry shelves gleam smooth.
But tonight Anuk will purr in her arms,
and she will dream of Northern Lights.

Poems Written During One Long Night

If I took everything with a grain of salt,
things would get salty real fast.

The Lonely Season

My loneliness is like water sliding down my throat.
Let it be the balm of Gilead, that bittersweet delight that keeps
my soul
from giving in.
My loneliness is like a silken noose that drapes my neck.
Let it be the garment that steels me
from the icy wind,
that cannot break my body,
only graze it with light.
My loneliness is like the tarmacs where planes never rest;
they touch and then take flight.
Let it be the launching pad for dreams,
brief respite for crafts that sweep the stars.
My loneliness is like a dead thing that I have never met,
and yet I moan its dying like my own
gentle death-
A drop reabsorbed into a vast sea
of crystal waters waiting to break free
of longing.
My loneliness is that song that weaves through winters,
the cry of wild geese in the summer breeze,
saying to its kind that winter will come again
and again
and again
and again
till the end of time. For everything
there is a season.

Irony

Everything is coming together,
and I am unhinged by
a righteous man,
so thoroughly hinged to Jesus
that I cannot get him down
from Heaven's Gate.
Though I try, I realize
I am batting for the wrong team,
guarding the other goal,
mixing my sports metaphors
and my priorities.
Like Yahtzee dice.
You do not follow me, but
I do.
This soft shifting means
the elevator of my life is about to descend
to new levels of bewilderment.
Fortunately, it must go up at some point.
And that jolly jolt
Will leave my stomach
flipping
like a pancake
in mid-air.
Bemused,
betwixt,
between,
belonging
in an instant
of recognition.

Heartbreak

Why does heartbreak
precede wisdom.
How about a heart *crack?*
A heart *ache?*
Why the break.
Why the break.
Take a crack, they say.
No, please don't.
I need that magic armor
to shelter me from the shattering of
dreams that were probably
unrealistic from the start,
as most are.
Holy Lord,
I'm dying.
You rose again.
Make the three days quick.
Nobody knows
how funny this is,
waiting for my heart
to heal again
so it can greet
the next arrow.
You think I'm exaggerating.

Ego

What can I say about you?
You are in everything I say
and do,
like arsenic in
my sandwich.
Why? What did I ever do
to you
but feed you? And wonder why
you grow?

Repentance

Loaded word. I said you once.
I said you thrice. I said you four times four repeating and still
don't mean it. Why
did I bother to say sorry?
How
will I know if I mean it
this time? My gun
is cocked at my head
(metaphorically speaking)
while I sing a theme song
then shout out "lifeline!"
How many lifelines
does it take
to get to the center
of a hypocrite?

Foolishness

I cannot separate you from regret.
You two are like mirror and image,
the kick, fall and echo,
the nickel in the well,
the crack of a bell,
the stucco makeup that makes us
recognizably human creatures of clay.
Who would I be
without my foolishness?
My mirror wants to know.

Refuge

Seeking solace in the arms
of a mortal man
is like finding refuge
in the wings of an ice angel.
Even the most beautiful will melt
or morph into unrecognizable creatures,
shedding cold and shiny tears.

Searching for happiness in the embrace
of the elite
is like trying to fly with the birds
of prey.
Majestic eagles will not catch
your fall,
only pierce you
with their talons.

Distractions can only
numb the pain
to the extent that reality
waits for your greeting.

Poetry

This is my song.
This is my Yolanda Adams gospel ballad,
my Celine Dion prodigy supra-phonographic rifts
cutting through the heavens
like a knife.
This is my statement,
my Marx, Mein Kampf, my Long Walk to something or other,
my legacy surviving me in questions
and in other people's perceptions.
This is my Titanic, my Katrina of its time.
My Mussolini, my Mother Teresa.
My greatest natural disaster and worst dictator.
My holiest human.My oxy-moron.
My clear testament to my confusion,
And not the last.
My America-centric liberal white manifesto
of uniqueness
amidst a million other
such manifestos
shouting
hear me! I am
special.
When I am lonely
my poems have a party
with me.
They keep me company.

After You Broke My Pain

Broken pain is like the tumbled walls of Babylon,
now overrun with wildflowers
clothed in all their beauty.

After you broke my pain, I saw so many colors,
I had to take slow steps,
down from the leaning towers
of self-defense now crumbling
into the all-embracing
earth of your kindness,
into the lushness of possibility,
the fertile promise of trust.

After you broke my pain, I knew it wasn't about
ever seeing you again,
but the seed you planted so tenderly in my heart
as if I belonged in this precious garden,
and as I grow, my fears continue to erode,
overrun by the wild joy of love's intricate design.

Go in Peace

How do I let you go,
precious angel God has sent?
Moments of Heaven in my heart
in those times our eyes have met.
Kindred spirit, holy heart,
trapped inside your human form.
You have shown me love transcends
each and every human norm.
How I wish that I could hold you,
but I know that love consists
in letting go of what you covet;
there can be no deeper kiss.
There is only one true meaning
living inside all of us;
how I look forward to the feeling:
no more pain, or greed, or lust.
How much I look forward to seeing
love unbridled, without fear.
Knowing you has been like healing;
you're a man whose sight is clear.
Now I close my eyes to longing,
now I lift my heart in song
in this chorus of belonging:
singing to the Holy One.
For how much lovelier is He
than this angel He has sent?

How much wiser is He
than this person he calls "friend"?
Look how kind my Father is,
taking time to send me someone.
Even if it's just in passing,
love's rays blind like burning sun,
searing away false perceptions
of importance, honor, fame,
prestige, power, pride and pleasure-
nothing matters but God's name.
Even if we only meet
just once in this brief shadowy world,
I know we will meet in Heaven;
you have led me to the Word.
So now go with all the blessings
this humbled child can profess.
Know that there can be no challenge
with His strength you cannot pass.
Know that you have been a blessing
to this daughter of our God.
You have moved me by confessing
your imperfect, false façade.
For if you can keep on going,
I know must do my best.
I am such a broken human,
but in God's pure strength I rest.

Poems written on the T

Who teaches us that gold is precious, and
when it's okay to smile?

My Heart's Not On My Sleeve

My heart's not on my sleeve.
It's miles ahead of me,
like a neon sign on a Vegas strip,
blinking: HIT ME!!!

Anatomy

My mind's DNA is a helix of metaphors,
my heart is a spiral of songs.
My blood the pulse of red rhythms,
my sinews long ribbons of stars,
my eyes 2 brown pools of perfection,
my feet instruments of prayer.
My fingers are made of light,
and my throat is a haven of birds.
My stomach is earthen and lush.
All creation takes flight through my words.

A Ballroom Dance with Gandhi

His waist is thin, hands sure.
Surprisingly strong when I dip,
hissvelte brown frame is clothed in
handmade white linen.
He doesn't sweat much.
There's a twinkle in his eye
and mischief in his smile.
He bows humbly when last violin cries.

Jacob's Wresting Match
Continued

Fear has me in its tight-fist grip.
I spend all my energy trying not to slip.
Supernatural means are needed to equip me
with tools to resist this perverse guilt trip.
Tell me the truth so I will not me moved.
Let all lies be rebuked so I will not be moved,
so I will know my worth, and that will break this curse,
and I will not desert, until the last is first,
until my face is true, until I talk to you.
I can't find words to say.
How do I talk to you?
I want to drop this ruse
so I can be brand new,
just like I was before.
I want to say "I do"
because it's life I choose.
Fears grip recoils from light.
This battle I won't lose.
Your supernatural might
has given me the tools
to overcome this fight.
I stand upon the truth.

True words

Empty words are vacant coffins.
False words are the kiss of death.
Your words are the act of loving.
Quicken me now with your breath.

New Mind

Give me a new mind.
Refine away the fears and turn my tears to peace.
Nothing is new, all things You have created.
Take me higher to a truer place.
Closer and closer to Your face.

We're All Virgins to the Joy

*"We're all virgins to the joy of loving without fear."-Janelle
Monae*

We're all virgins to the joy of loving without fear.
We're all hazy in the dawn before the day turns clear.
If only we could pause, and heal
the pain that comes from knowing without feeling.
If only we could stop, and see
the kind of sight that comes from beyond seeing.

A Poem Written During One Long Summer

The summer of 2010.

Samaritan

I am building a tower that matters on sand,
speaking a language I don't understand,
wielding a whip of deceit in my hand,
making you lug Lego bricks up a ramp,
locking you up in concentration camps,
Samaritan.

I tell you "dream of Heaven," but I'm sleeping.
I bid you sow my seeds, but when I reap them,
I see that I am Judas and the prodigal son,
watching the sea claim my Lego pipe dream.

I brought you to Egypt; I sold you as slaves.
Now I see a great light just before waves
crash upon me, washing the mud from my eyes.
Ocean of wine,
drunk with a love so divine,
that you would bleed to quench my thirst,
and die to salve my hunger.

For I follow your light like a star in the night,
up into Freedom's Kingdom.
Away from the lies I was living,
back to when I was thinking I could kill you,
which would be to stab out my eyes and sever my limbs,
'cause His Light is shining in us,

and we're not comprehending.

Samaritan,
oh woman at the well,
oh in my toga of denim, I fell.
I thought I was king; why do you drop your stones?
Don't you know I will throw them in your face,
let you die in disgrace
for adultery?
While I sleep with Messrs. Nasdaq and Dow Jones.
I throw you some crumbs, heifers and micro-loans.
I'm bowing to phalluses dripping with gold,
thinking size matters
in matters of soul.
Bought and sold,
my body the temple
of his greed.
"Sacred" and scared-just a flip of the "c."
Entitled to me, he scoffs at my needs,
and I let him define what it means to succeed.
I tolerate, he segregates, denying our truth:
our common humanity,
given to vanity
driven to insanity.
Fear-based hoarding mentality
leveraging status, designing morality
to suit our own purposes; we don't know that Truth is
the One who created us loves and forgives.

Missing pieces inside, His Kingdom denied,
from you I hide and your value deride.
If I dropped my pride then I would abide
in you, and you in me.

I'm so blind, I'm inclined to define you by me.
Black bodies hanging from the poplar trees
I don't see; it's not me.
I'm in charge, and I'm free
Could it be, the One and unchanging Truth
that in us He designed eternal clues
to the puzzle of how we fit together?
Dislocated, refugees
trying desperately to cling
to material things.
Let freedom ring
for those with degrees
inherit the earth
yet fall to their knees.
If I ever think that I hold the keys
to the Kingdom,
I'm so dumb,
my brain numb,
in fiefdom.
I'm just a salt column,
'cause Sodom comes undone.
I'm a corpse made of pride,
and He gives me true Life,
bleeding to death just to open my eyes.
I was sleeping here, dreaming that I was the king
over everyone
and everything.
Watching gold idols on TV fling bling,
roving through Amazon, buying dead things,
eating my brothers like Idi Amin.
I killed more Armenians than the Sultan,
before the cock crowed, I thrice denied them,
made you think that you were broken,

MKULTRA, Arti-chokin'.
Guns smoking, keep hoping.
The history books so thin,
their stories unwritten,
drugged populations,
manipulation,
sedation, massive surveillance,
Jesus is Haitian.
Iran-Contra invasion,
so-called "free" elections.
Michelob Ultra . . .
dontchawanna
buy the things that make you hot?
'Cause it's so obvious you're not
good enough
without this stuff.
Buy some sex; it's just like love
without the fuss.
Yes, you can trust
the Fed
It knows what's best for us.
(We're dead),
wearing our underwear on our heads,
going to Payless to buy Keds,
can't accept a world with no debt,
watching kids die on the TV set,
closing our ears when we need to repent.
Oh Mother Africa,
bathing in paprika,
wading through toxins so I can buy sneakers.
Don't wanna hear, denial cuts off my ear,
like Judas in the garden.
What's that you say? Pardon?

You can't find Osama?
All of England on camera.
Echelon, Frenchelon,
gray fields of Babylon,
electric sheep dreaming on,
where have all the Kennedys gone?
Inconvenient truths made R. Helms aloof.
Camp Hero, Ground Zero, Simple Lie groups.
Anti-gravity, LSD,
just try to discredit me.
Don't know much about physics but
this is my m-theory:
Maker and matter, magnificent mystery.
I don't understand but I know it's our destiny.
Divinity's in us, yet lies get the best of me.
My mind's so material, surrendering sets me free.
Mercy ethereal, Love with us, Miracle,
100% real and 100% metaphor,
ever-expanding, never-changing,
infinitely dimensional,
everlasting fractals and glories intentional.
Heaven surrounds us.
We can't hear the sounds of
the One who designed us:
sweet music of silence,
Magnificent Kindness,
our common divineness.
Surrender unbinds us, gives
freedom from blindness.
Forgive me for mindlessly
feeding electric sheep,
leaving your lambs to weep
Must I my brother keep?

Jamie Zwiebel

Passed him by in the street.
Samaritan, let us now leave this Babylon.
Holy ground all around
from Lagos to Saigon.
It's finished by the Son.
Take up your mats and run.
Zion surrounds us.
It's already done.

"Samaritan" References

Arti-chokin' CIA operation called Operation ARTICHOKE which researched interrogation methods and was forerunner to MKULTRA. The scope of the project was outlined in a memo dated January 1952 that stated, "Can we get control of an individual to the point where he will do our bidding against his will and even against fundamental laws of nature, such as self-preservation?"

Babylon Psalm 137:2-5, Isaiah 14:21-23, Isaiah 21:8-13, Isaiah 39:5-7, Isaiah 13:19, Isaiah 43:13-15, Isaiah 47:1-3, Isaiah 48:13-21, Jeremiah 20:5-7, Jeremiah 21:1-11, Jeremiah 24:1-3, Jeremiah 25:11-13, Jeremiah 27:17-22, Jeremiah 28:1-14, Jeremiah 29:3-11, Jeremiah 36:28-30, Jeremiah 42:11, Jeremiah 50 especially Jeremiah 50:28, Jeremiah 51, Ezekiel 17:11-20, Ezekiel 21:1-22, Daniel 3, Micah 4:9-11, Zechariah 2:6-8, Acts 7:42-44, Revelation 16:18-20, Revelation 17:4-6, Revelation 18:1-22, Revelation 19:1-3.

black bodies hanging from the poplar trees refers to Billie Holiday song, "Strange Fruit."

Bought and sold, my body the temple of his greed, sacred and scared just a flip of the 'c' Matthew 6:24, John 8:38-45, John 4:15-21.

Camp Hero a military base in Montauk Point, New York.

Dislocated, refugees, trying desperately to cling to material things Genesis 11, Exodus 33, Matthew 19, Mark 10, Luke 18.

Echelon a signals intelligence collection and analysis network operated on behalf of the five signatory states to the UK-USA Security Agreement (Australia, Canada, New Zealand, the United Kingdom, and the United States).

Electric sheep <u>Do Androids Dream of Electric Sheep?</u>, a science fiction novel by American writer Philip K. Dick first published in 1968.

Fractals infinitely complex self-similarity.

Frenchelon French part of Echelon.

Idi-Amin a military leader and President of Uganda from 1971-1979.

I'm a corpse made of pride, and He gives me true life 1 Corinthians 13:8.

I'm so blind, I'm inclined to define you by me. John 2:10-11.

It's already done Jeremiah 31:3, John 19:29-31.

Iran-Contra In the mid 1980s, senior officials in the administration of American President Reagan secretly facilitated the sale of arms to Iran, the subject of an arms embargo, to secure the release of American hostages and allow U.S. intelligence agencies to fund the Nicaraguan Contras, an opposition group which overthrew the administration of democratically elected Nicaraguan President Daniel Ortega.

Judas in the garden Matthew 26:46-48.

Killed more Armenians The deliberate and systematic destruction of the Armenian population of the Ottoman Empire during and just after World War I.

Kingdom, the North star which African-American slaves followed to freedom, Luke 17:20-21.

Leaving your lambs to weep John 21:14-16, Luke 10:2-4, Isaiah 16:1-3, Isaiah 40:10-12.

Light Isaiah 62:1, John 1:1-5, John 3:24, John 8:12.

"Missing pieces inside, His Kingdom denied, from you I hide and your value deride. If I dropped my pride then I would abide in you, and you in me." John 14:18-27, John 17:11-26, Colossians 3:12-15.

MKULTRA the code name for a covert, illegal human research program run by the CIA from the early 1950s, continuing at least through the late 1960s, which used U.S. and Canadian citizens as its test subjects in over 150 research projects designed to explore any possibilities of mind control.

m-theory a single underlying theory which purposes to unite and supersede each of the five super string theories.

Must I my brother keep? Passed him by in the street. Genesis 4, Luke 10.

The prodigal son Luke 15.

R. Helms Richard Helms was the Director of the CIA from 1966-1973. In 1972, he ordered the destruction of most of the records of the MKULTRA project. He was the only director to have been convicted of lying to the United States Congress over CIA undercover activities.

Samaritan Matthew 10:4-6, Luke 9:50-53, Luke 10:33, Luke 17:16, John 4:1-10, John 4:21-23, John 4:38-41, John 8:48, Acts 8:25.

Simple Lie Groups a theory of continuous symmetry of mathematical objects and structures in abstract algebra whose only ideals are 0 and itself.

Sodom Genesis 19, Isaiah 13:19.

take up your mats John 5:7-9, Luke 7:21-23.

"Those with degrees inherit the earth yet fall to their knees" Matthew 5:4-6, 1 Corinthians 13:8, Psalm 37:8-12, 1 Samuel 2:7-9, Jeremiah 16:18-20, Psalm 82:7-8.

watching the sea claim my Lego pipe dream Exodus 14, Surah 26: 60-67.

when the cock crowed, I thrice denied them Mark 14, Matthew 26 and 27.

why do you drop your stones? John8, Romans 2:1, Matthew 7:1, Deuteronomy 17:7

woman at the well John 4.

Zion Psalm 126:1-3, Psalm 132:13, 133:2-3, Psalm 143:2-3, Psalm 137:1-4, 3:15-18, Isaiah 12:5-6, Isaiah 14:31-32, Isaiah 16:1-3, Isaiah 18:6-7, Isaiah 29:7-9, Isaiah 30:19, Isaiah 31:3-5, Isaiah 31:9, Isaiah 33:13-15, Isaiah 33:20, Isaiah 35:10, Isaiah 37:22, Isaiah 37:32, Isaiah 40:9, Isaiah 59:20, Isaiah 60:13-15, Isaiah 61:3, Isaiah 62:10, Isaiah 66:7-9, Jeremiah 3:14, Jeremiah 6:23, Jeremiah 8:19, Jeremiah 30:16-18, Jeremiah 31:12, Jeremiah 50:5, Jeremiah 50:28, Lamentations 4:22, Joel 2:1, Joel 2:32, Joel 3:15-18, Amos 6:1, Obadiah 1:16-21, Micah 1:12-14, Micah 3:9-11, Micah 4, Zephaniah 1:13.

> *"All the art that I supposedly create*
> *is simply a faded reflection of something He's already made."*
> *-Lacey Sturm, 1 Corinthians 13:12*